LOVE OR SUICIDE
AND
THE LIFE IN-BETWEEN

Written by James S M Parker

Grosvenor House
Publishing Limited

All rights reserved
Copyright © James S M Parker, 2012

James S M Parker is hereby identified as author of this
work in accordance with Section 77 of the Copyright, Designs
and Patents Act 1988

The book cover picture is copyright to James S M Parker

This book is published by
Grosvenor House Publishing Ltd
28-30 High Street, Guildford, Surrey, GU1 3EL.
www.grosvenorhousepublishing.co.uk

This book is sold subject to the conditions that it shall not, by way of
trade or otherwise, be lent, resold, hired out or otherwise circulated
without the author's or publisher's prior consent in any form of binding or
cover other than that in which it is published and
without a similar condition including this condition being imposed
on the subsequent purchaser.

A CIP record for this book
is available from the British Library

ISBN 978-1-78148-542-2

'...and to all the lovers and to all those who see the world for what it is and what it could be..."

My Michelle, put simply...thank you.

What's in it (my heart)

0 Introduction 1   1. This is... 4
2. Destroy Create 6   3. Love 7   4. Suicide 8
5. The Little Things That Make Love (part 1) 9
6. From The Darkest Reaches 10
7. An Ode To Absinthe 11
8. The Room 12   9. Darkness 14   10. Search 15
11. A Song 16
12. A Song 17
13. ALONE 18
14. Alone 20
15 Epic 21   16. Aftermath? 22
17. Fight For IT 24
18. The Little Things That Make Love (part 2) 26
19. Love or suicide 27   20. Matters! 29   21. Inside 30
22. What BinDs US 31
23. The Kiss of Dreams 32
24. Wish 33   25. DamagED 34   26. To Be Or Not To Be 35
27. fEEling...tHOught 36
28. HATEEEE 37
29. A DiFFerencE 38
30. Destiny 40   31. The Little Things That Make Love (part 3) 41
32. Shoulders 42
33. The Joy of Suicide 43
34. That First Kiss 44   35. What my dad did to my mum 45
36. Revenge 46
37. With Me 47
38. SUDDENLY 48   39. The Little Things That Make Love (part 4) 49
40. I... 50
41. Lonely World 51   42. Mirror Image egamI rorriM 52
43. An Experiment? 53

44. A JOKE 54   45. The Little Things That Make Love (part 5) 55
    46. ??????? 56   47. ???? 57
            48. forevER 58
                                    49. 100 59
    50. Useful Quotes 60   51. GENeticcc 62
  52. How Can Anyone Listen???? 63   53. DREAm 64
54. StatistIC 65
55. Love Is 66   56. Care For Me 68   57. Fly With Them///////////// 69
                58. Black 70
              59. Dear Dad 71
                60. PG 72
          61. The Continuation Of Nothing 73
            62. M(ultiple)umS(clerosis) 75
                63. The Diner 76
            64. A Verse From The heart 78
                65. Hurt 79
              66. Once Upon A Time 80
                67. A Dead Home 82
                  68. Point? 83
69. THE NOTE 84
                                    70. THE END 85

Introduction

Life is hard…for every single one of us. We all experience good things. We all experience bad things. We lose people. We make stupid decisions. We regret things. We love. We hate. We live.

My Father was a bad man. He was bad to my Mother. He loved to drink more than he should have. He ran off with another woman using the excuse he couldn't look after my Mother who had Multiple Sclerosis. Like I said, he was a bad man.

My Mother was a saint. She worked as a nurse. She taught and helped people. She was a good Mother. Her only crime was loving my Father, which she did, right till the end.

The disease eventually killed my Mother. It had taken away her ability to walk, feed herself, clean herself, have any sort of life…it even took away her ability to speak. I watched her die - heard her very last breath and saw her slip away.

The book you hold in your hands was a direct response to me dealing with my Father's actions and my Mother's death and it was fuelled by lager, whisky and later,

Absinthe. I was lonely, angry and lost. Long drunken nights were spent digging deeper and deeper into the darker side of my soul which came pouring out onto the page, uncensored and unedited.

I had never experienced love and I was spending more and more time thinking about suicide. My life felt completely empty and black, my body was being crushed by a dark void and my mind was in a wild emotional state, switching between mood swings and many contradictions every moment of every day.

But I got through it. Thanks to this book. It listened. It took everything I could give it and is a piece of work I am extremely proud of. This is really the point of it. It isn't a manual on how to commit suicide or a glorification on the dark aspects of life. Or even an ideal look on love and all its inner trappings. It is simply an extremely honest collection of thoughts and emotions I experienced whilst going through a really tough period in my life. And it should be read that way. If you, the reader, is feeling suicidal or lost, then my advice is to get it all out. Be that on the page, through a guitar, to a Doctor or loved one, or on a blank canvas; just get it out. You only get one chance in life and it should never be discarded through suicide.

Nowadays, nearly 10 years since I completed this book, I am in a much better place. I haven't touched a drop of alcohol in 6 years, am in a loving relationship with my Michelle, have a steady full time job and am having continued success with my writing through competitions and various websites. Not only that, I have seen, heard, read, played and experienced amazing things and will continue to do so.

Of course, the darkness will always be there, it will never go - but it will never win.

James S M Parker – 09/06/12.

This is...

Visions of hate from so called neighbourly love
Destruction from within, lies tainted with lies
Truth felt in-between violence swamped in joy
Stink follows stink, musty, sweet, rotten
Twisted nightmares dream other nightmares
A small boy becomes a rapist, sadist
An old woman becomes a washed in pain, cleansed
Metal through metal and twins fall
The tool of knowledge perverted mirrored
Is a graveyard of innocence filed under paedo
Animals tortured kept alive as playthings
Their insides out, trampled and worn
Horizons are scorched and erased, bled dry
The bones of the Earth now a fog of ash and what was
A timeless portrait of cracked colour fading
Reworked by the feathered shadows of suicide
Burning distortions, deafening choirs grinning certainty
The compass of fear and rage directed inward
Deceased thoughts decayed and cruel, vile, horrid
Beaten compassion violated and forced apart
Raw flesh lightens the darkness, taints the air
Poisons minds of purity melting eyes of midnight tears
Slaughter follows defecation erotic sick ejaculation
Seeds of famine injected through canals of hunger
Deep into heart of black, shrivelled and hurt, deep

Open wounds crawl and suffocate, splashed, thick
Bodies sold and used, broken and begging, ripped
Stitched together with stone and button skin
Slowly infecting sanity becoming inner epidemic
Addicting souls drawn to a blood fever
An overdose of abominations damning, damned
And blistered, shattered, a cursed reflection
By our own demented arrogance, dead and blind
Lost and alone, bad and worse this is…this is…
The day the whole world went away.

Destroy
Create

Which

                                        Is

     easier???????????

               They say it is easier to destroy than create!!!

                                             Love
                                           suicide.....

Now what do they say????????????????????????????????
???????????

Love

Wars have been won and lost
And for what? Time has been destroyed
While money is god. And for what?
Stars have been named and shamed
As the air itself becomes substance
And for what…is this thing called love?

An eternity or a fleeting glimpse! Why ask me?
You should know, or is it a privilege
Enjoyed by the beautiful people…the beautiful people
Impossible! A man made feeling, screaming, peeling
Away that certain someone
Is love the core? The final door?

What if it comes at a price? If love itself…
Can love itself be owned by one, exclusively?
Should true love conquer all…that's good?
And be held back, caged for the right reasons
Because it belongs to another. And for what…
Is this thing called love? Right time, right place!

Suicide

Slicing skin night time red
underneath my bed time said
it experience life, sore head
craving bullshit we are fed
innocence faded I am led
deep inside the land of the dead
except wait, I forgot ted.

The Little Things That Make Love (part 1)

It's the little things that make love
The big things anyone can do
But the little things that make love
Are reserved for me and you

The connection between the eyes
And the counting of the fingers
All lead to the ultimate sighs
What's that? The angel singers.

From The Darkest Reaches

A place no one should go
Beyond even hell itself
Have you been? You would remember!
Seeing things you never thought possible
Hearing words that would cause
blisters on those who spoke them
A horrid place, an evil place, yet...
We all go there from time to time
because it lies in us all...
from the darkest reaches.

(Dark Green!!!)

An Ode To Absinthe

An innocent looking drink yet
Never one to trust

Over the hills and far away
Desert land awaits
Entertainment as visions

To lead us into complete madness
Or absolute joy

And world inspiration
But drink in modesty
Saviour the warmth
It can easily take over
No! It can easily destroy
The weak minded and foolish
Hell welcomes them while
Extremities flood over us.

The Room

'THE ROOM' is darkly lit by your smell
Intensifying to breaking point
We undress. Slowly and deliberately
Eyes locked, bodies on heat
The air fills with music, natural music
And we move closer. That first touch
Skin on skin. Exploring. Time has no meaning
Your body becomes my work of art
As I mould every line, over and over
Making my way. Eventually across your neck
Down over perfect breasts
Smoothing through navel and hips
Yet jumping…down towards silky legs
Squeezing the calf muscle, I can tell
Your body squirms for release. Yet I hold back
Listening to your panting. I kiss your feet
Slightly tickling your soul. You laugh. I smile
Now I move to the centre. Parting
My tongue dances. And tastes
My fingers swim. And drown
You buckle. I speed up. And we are lost
Beyond love. Beyond pleasure. Beyond hope
I watch. And I drink
You bite. And you empty
And I pause, hearts pound

As I turn you over onto your front
Running my finger across curved spine
Jumping, again, to kiss the back of your legs
While scratching your glistening back
I stop. And ask your permission
You give it and I move to the centre. Parting
This time slowly and gentle
The taste is different. The reaction though…the same
The feeling intensifies. You arch. I cry
And the moment is ours. Forever
The night is alive. The room free
And we share…everything
From the inside out.

Darkness

Colours have gone, frightened away
Forced by my hand…they say
Darkness sweeps above my head
A gradual decline…they said

Eyes grow dim and lifeless
Drums fill the nothingness
Whistling rings through my ears
Cries of help…no one hears

The mind becomes oh so dumb
Fingers to the touch? Numb
Limbs decide to go limp
Emotionless becomes your pimp

Then comes the loneliness
Always it makes such a mess
Imploding frustration backfires
Snapping the piano wires

And it's far too late
As all fear turns to hate
And the light is lost forever
Amongst the black feather
And I am gone more or less
Never to defeat the darkness.

Search

I caught that blank look in the mirror, my glasses reflecting reflections as shadows fill the craters on my skin and pinhole stubble darkens an even darker past. Lips cracked and split are motionless with only a sliver of stained teeth exposed. A skimmer of light shines on an even shinier nose revealing black hole nostrils stuffed with spider's legs. The lobes of my ears flap as sizes vary from side to side, dead hair seems alive thanks to 2 in 1 yet sits lifeless atop a beaten mound of skull. Veins, wrinkles and inner scars litter a forehead of violence and pain while eyebrows of dust frame expressions of nothingness. Bruised coloured bags encase eyes of night, pupils darker than glass rimmed by a muddy moon swimming in balls of milk. I search. I search for the feelings to exist, they must be here somewhere!

A Song

A butterfly soars through the forest rain

Who had far too much time on his hands?

She seemed exposed in all of me

My fall will be for you

My love will be for you

I get all numb when she sings

Oh girlfriend, follow me into my darkness

The clown with a condition of the heart

This is the one song in heaven

In my dreams there's a corner for me and you

Still broken wings can't keep me down

You know I love you

Moonlight

Save me.

A Song

In solitude I can't deal with my own existence

Cause life's unreal and you're living a lie

Death of god. Death of feeling

What a fantastic death this is

What a fantastic death abyss

Lonely without mommy's love

Down to the very last breath

When you're talking to yourself and nobody's listening

It will all come crashing down in desperation

Could anybody love me? Or is it just a crazy dream

(too much blood for such a tiny hole)

Dark night of my soul…

Time to die.

ALONE

I
GO
NOW
TO
EXIST
IN
DEATH
WHAT
I
WAS
IN
LIFE
...
ALONE,
SO
ALONE.

I
GO
NOW
TO
EXIST
IN
DEATH
WHAT

I
WAS
IN
LIFE
...
ALONE,
SO
ALONE.

I
GO
NOW
TO
EXIST
IN
DEATH
WHAT
I
WAS
IN
LIFE
...
ALONE,
SO
ALONE.

Alone

The silence around me screams
Thoughts mean nothing to anyone
(cause no one is here)
Puppet teddies stare and laugh
A fly breaks the sound barrier
(until the spider catches it)
Television reflections shadow me
Bulbs are the only sign of life
(hot and bright for a while)
I sit still and vacant
Wondering why I am still alone
(always in an offhand way)
Racing answers flash my mind
Fill my empty heart up
(leaving room for a glimmer of hope)
Ghosts of reasons deafen me
A charade of self-pity
(and of fear and loathing)
An hour passes and I am older
My failings wrinkle within
(but not to the naked eye)
And I am left with no reflection
No reason, no time
(cause times up).

Epic

Then I return from that place,
back once more.
I peer long and hard at my face
in through the out-door.

Eyes like black holes,
breathing pounding drums.
A tortured bag of souls,
tossed with a fraction of sums.

Salted beads of wet,
crawl free from their cells.
Movement restricted yet,
ears ringing of bells.

The fear becomes ever so apparent,
manifested through shivers and shakes.
Memory loss a heaven sent,
an embarrassment awakes.

And then comes the promise,
to give up the drink for good.
Like a fateful non-existent kiss,
or the true thickness of blood.

Aftermath?

The phone rang but there was no one to pick it up.
           That is not to say that the room was empty…it wasn't!
    A smell filled it from top to bottom and it oozed through every crack, every single nail hole into the bricks; sodden and musk.

           The phone stopped and took its message. An upset woman on the other line said something like 'are you ok?' and 'no one has seen you in weeks!' and 'why haven't you been in work?'
    (**something** along those lines anyways)

This was the sixth message of its ilk. None of the messages were replied to, but there was a very good reason for that. A *very, very* good reason for that. It was murky inside the room and stained…forever. Not to say that it was a mess, in fact the total opposite.

He had given his room a spring clean before...there was no one to answer the phone and even though it was the middle of winter,
the room was as warm as a fluffy sunshiny day.

This scene that awaited anyone was as random as random does and unique in its execution.

Anyone who entered would never forget or want to remember. That was his point. That was his reason for living, his meaning of life...and death. Good on him.

The phone rang one last time
                      There was no one to pick it up.......

Fight For IT

IF YOU EVER FIND LOVE FIGHT FOR

IT FOREVER.

OK!!!!!!!

The Little Things That Make Love (part 2)

The scent of the hair
And the touching of the toes
A pair of eyes so rare
Compared to a red red rose

The gaze into the soul
Makes time itself stand still
Please fill up my bowl
And take hold of my will.

Love or suicide

Love or suicide
Black or white
Good or bad
Left or right
Hot or cold
Bath or shower
Male or female
Drink or drugs
Sister or brother
Mother or father
Family or friend
Night or day
Long or short
Film or tele
Pen or pencil
Dark or light
Cat or dog
House or flat
Wet or dry
Smooth or rough
Life or death
Wee or pooh
Deaf or blind
Arm or leg
Smell or taste

Pub or club
Original or special edition
Computer or console
Read or write
Sceptic or believer
Drawing or painting
Gay or straight
Number or letter
Guitar or keyboard
Photo or memory
Car or bike
Work or play
Genius or idiot
Naked or clothed
Dick or vagina
Beginning or end
and the life in-between.

Matters!

I

waaannnnnnnnnnnaaaa

DDDDOOOOOOooooo

SUm………………..……………………………………..thing

that,.,.,.,.,.,.,.,.,.,.,.,.,.,.

Matters!

Inside

Inside empty perfection
Lies a beauty in state
An untouched, unspoiled dream
Surrounding my unworthy hands
Diluting my sodden mind
Collapsing my guarded heart

Inside an empty perfection
Lies a tunnel in state
A vision of stubbornness, fickle
Guiding my wandering eyes
Levelling my uncertain fate
Revealing my captured path

Inside empty perfection
Lies a love in state
An endless, chronic feeling
Tainting my ugly touch
Upsetting my classified norm
Perfecting my empty inside.

What BinDs US

.that remember .back own its gets it ,sometimes .lid eye an batting without home blue big our of wrists the cut we .day every dry earth the bleed we .itself planet the fed now it and body his from drained had it when earth the of part become had blood his .get would he best the is man dead a to which…nothing was had he all ,hope no and go to place no ,identity no had he .earth the to him bound blood his but .hell to straight gone have should he rights by-sin a considered ,beliefs some in ,is suicide as .case the always is as himself blamed he .him to next… sleep her in…died just she .accident an in die didn't she and murdered wasn't she .died life his of love the because this did he .drain himself watched and wrists his cut he .suicide committed had he after long earth the on wandered man a .both do can blood .us destroy can us binds what (start here)

Us Binds What

The Kiss of Dreams

Lost, alone just she and I…
all else a blur except for her.
But it doesn't matter where we are,
and it doesn't matter what we are doing,
because nothing distracts and nothing compares.

Her eyes; small as they are,
are big enough to keep me safe,
open enough to know me, hold me, feed me.
And as she smiles, the weight lifts,
darkness lightens and hope laughs,
while her touch marks my skin as we inch closer
…so close.

I can smell the life in her breath,
hear the strings of her heart play,
and we stop…and we listen…

> our symphony sings
> our meaning found
> the kiss of dreams
> our destiny bound.

Wish

To wake up by a kiss

And a smile, eyes penetrating

Through my heart and into my soul

The endless silence of a beat

Sparks when we meet

A wish of a dream I have

One that will never be

To wake up by a kiss.

DamagED

JU s t

                         hhooowwwwwwwwwwww

dammmmmageddd

                     have

      I

    BE come……………………………………………..

    from this mundane

??……………………

                                well?

To Be Or Not To Be

As by day, my life is swamped with the mundane,
The 9-5 monthly wage drives me insane.
But when freedom comes and I escape,
I run home, unlock my brain and create!

Working on characters both butcher and pig,
Giving voices to the 'shut up!'
Sonatas to the mute, eyesight to the blind,
An orchestra to the deaf deafens, builds,
And keeps the dead walking, the living running.

Time has no teeth, no rules to speak of,
Elements are vulgar and bold, extravagant!
While no animals are harmed in my typo,
Emotions are punctuated, capital led and Q-M'd.
Twists become the norm, words made up,
And description waltzes, elegant and beautiful,
Painful and joyful…the end.

As by night, my life is of no importance,
It's my fingertips that are free to dance.
Because all it takes is a single word,
And suddenly, as if by magic, my characters are heard.

fEEling...tHOught

`1234567890-=
qwertyuiop[]
asdfghjkl;'#
\zxcvbnm,./
IF LOVE COMES FROM THE HEART
THEN SUICIDE COMES FROM THE HEAD
ONE IS A FEELING
THE OTHER A THOUGHT
LIFE
DEATH
`1234567890-=
qwertyuiop[]
asdfghjkl;'#
\zxcvbnm,./
WHAT IF LOVE BECAME THE THOUGHT
AND SUICIDE THE FEELING
WOULD IT MAKE A DIFFERENCE
\zxcvbnm,./
asdfghjkl;'#
qwertyuiop[]
`1234567890-=

HATEEEE

                                        FOUnd

soooooooooooooooooo

                            many

                way""""'"sss

  tOOO

                                            hate

            MySeLLLfffffffffffffffff………………..

  excuse

                    follllow'S

EXcuSE

      HATE

                HATTTTEEERRRRHATTEE

      OOHH my.

A DiFFerencE

If
*Heaven
Or
Hell
Were
Proven
To
Exist
.
Would
The
Suicide
Rate
Go
Down
?
Would
We
All
Become
A
Peaceful
Race
?
Or*

*Would
It
Even
Make
A
Difference*
?

.

What
Do
You
Think
?

.
.
.
.
.
.
.
.
.
.
.
.

Destiny

When I look in the mirror and see me,
do I see me, or am I he?
Does destiny begin with a dee?
Or am I in fact the one; he?

Purple lamps shade on the porch,
the blackness of his heart pumps! Pumps what?
Blood! No, it can't be, it shouldn't be,
he! Speakers fuse the air with words.
Oh, what sweet words.

Lies, lies, heart pumps lies, for I
much better than he never to face
his destiny.

When I look in the mirror and see me,
Yes! I see me, an opposite to he,
my own destiny.

~~DAD~~

The Little Things That Make Love (part 3)

The warmth of your skin
And the darkness of your breath
Oh sweet deadly sin
Embrace alien death

The meeting of our bodies
Suffocate my mind
A mutual question please
Little things we find.

Shoulders

Love   and   suicide

Sit   either   side

of

    your
                        shoulderssssssssssssssssssssss

    (like a devil and an angel)))))

        Which

OnE111111111111111111111111111111111111111111111
1111111111111111111

                        DO you

            listen to the most???????????????

The Joy of Suicide

I am dead. I did myself in. Bleach and vodka. I am happy. I have no bills left to pay, no house to run, no bullshit job to go to, no expectations to fill, no pain. I don't have to shit anymore or be around people that bore me...believe me, there are a lot more interesting people where I am now. Limbo it's called, fuck, it still beats where I was any day. I am finally content.

My body doesn't need maintaining or cleaning.

I am never tired or ill. I never have to exercise (not that I ever did) or eat. It is like being on holiday. Time has no meaning or power. I am free from the things that bind you to your world. And who in their right mind wants to be bound to a place controlled by money. The joy of suicide is the way. The joy of suicide is the way. The joy of suicide is the way?

That First Kiss

I am so nervous looking at you
Waiting for an eternity, an experience new
Walls bleed hot sweet liquid
This day would never come, I once said.

But we are here facing each other
Anyone looking would see…I love her
And for once the feeling is the same
Countless near misses? Too many to name.

It begins to rain, what I'm not sure
Smiling though it sounds so pure
Years of loneliness never will I miss
Everything is lost in that first kiss.

What my dad did to my mum

See you
Impress you
Bullshit you
Own you
Fuck you
Cheat you
Rob you
Insult you
Leave you
Beg you
Turn you
Beat you
Fuck you
Complete you

Need me
Worship me
Give me

Fuck it

Leave you

And they call this love.

Revenge

A feeling not to be felt! Taking over my mind's eye
Drumbeats force into my blood, colour-blind said I
For black and white is easier to define, easier to die
Questions are not what I need. Please don't ask why?

A single meaningless thought! Obviously my destiny
Born to do this one thing, to keep the devil company
And words are not good enough to change my sympathy
Furious angel's actions become the revenge in me.

A deed already done! Far too late for regret
Loneliness is my reward, to give up is my not yet
One last thing I must do and suicide my debt
Scraping the barrel of excuses captured by my own net.

With Me

What do I see in your eyes?
Those frightened mirrors staring at me
Why do I see pain flashing by?
And empty thoughts out to sea

I can help if you only trust
For I have been to a place you go
Alone not lonely did I must
Deep through the twilight snow

Take my hand and hear my breath
Feel my warm sympathy
Not a chance has the death
While you hold onto thee

What do I see in your eyes?
Those frightened mirrors staring at me
New hope and love are flashing by
No empty thoughts out to sea.

SUDDENLY

my life doesN'T

SeEm

such a waste

IT ALL

revolves

around

????.

The Little Things That Make Love (part 4)

Every kiss screams divine
And brings its own intent
We commit erotic crime
With all seconds meant

The little things become big
As you sing chorus of love
Deep through each other we dig
Wings spread covering from above.

I...

I lost my love. My life is worthless without her. I cannot go on living. I will commit suicide. I..........................
....

Lonely World

I talk to myyyyyyy   owN shadow

Laugh   (ha ha ha ha ha ha ha ha ha ha) AT my OWn   jokes

feel for my own feelinGs

TouCH   my own SKIN

NO   one   comFOrTs   me wHen I NEed
                comforting

no   one   kiSSes   ME   wHen I need to BEE
                Kissed

NO   one   ListeNs   when IIIIIII neeeeed to beeeee
                hEARd

I have no-----------------------one   Who drEAm""""'s about ME

Or   wwwwwwiLLLLLL nOTice
                                    WHHen I am GOne

my heart beats

YeTT   TherE   is nO   one   TO TUNE   iT

My EYes seeeeeeeeeeeeeeeeeeeeee
                    allllllllllllll..................They SEEEee is mE

I liVEE   in THIS   world

I have no one who lives with me.........LoNEly wORLD...

Mirror Image egamI rorriM

How can people smile and be happy? Cause they have someone to come home to. It doesn't matter if it's a wife or a husband or a sister or a brother or a mother or a father or even just a friend. As long as there is someone there. Ready to hear about your day, ready to put a smile on your face, a spring in your step. It's hard to come home to find that the only face you will see tonight is the one reflected in the mirror. It becomes even harder when it is the same reflection night after night. And as the nights become years, the reflection seems alien, unnatural, a mirror image of the person that you were, seen through your own eyes and twisted to fit the demon within.

An Experiment?

I wonder what it feels like? To feel your blood drain, and feel your life slip. If I could cut my wrists then I phoned for an ambulance, would it be classed as a real suicide attempt? I want to know. I want to feel. What if I do it under supervision? Like that film. You know the one I mean. Then I could write about it. Have a better understanding of suicide. But would I? People would say that I was sick for doing such a thing just to write about it. Fuck them. Fuck you. What if the ambulance didn't come in time? Where would I go? Hell? Heaven? Any place is better than where I am at the moment. Is it too risky? What would I get out of it? Maybe I would learn to appreciate my life and choose to find love. Or maybe I would decide that it felt good. Imagine that. I could get a rush out of attempting suicide. I could do it in so many different ways, finding new and erotic things to kill myself with and then…be brought back…just so I could write about it. It would be one hell of a book; the pros and cons of suicide. I would become a living tapestry of suicide…scars of an experiment.

A JOKE

Knock knock
Who's there?
Soul
Soul who?
Soul mate!

If only it were that easy!!!!!!!!!!!!!!!!

The Little Things That Make Love (part 5)

The ice melting on the chest
With the water collecting down below
Intense beating from my breast
As dark as the carrion crow

And we soar as high as can be
Through clouds soaked in wine
Deep into our minds we can see
Pure love that screams divine.

???????

Something had happened tonight
The air was soggy and sour
Clouds were violent, roaring with glee
As the flashes of white exploded like war
And illuminated this sepia landscape

Wildlife was silent, cars...rare
While humanity lived a blur
On this night

Wind whispered a clear warning
Only understood by the lucky few
Has the green grass ever looked so red?
Some would say stained, until morning

A morning that, for one, will never arrive

Litter danced, road signs marched
Street lamps winked, fences stretched
A rubber ball escaped
And a siren cried a note of loss
Another life had broken and given up

No one noticed...or cared
Except the Angels
Those weeping Angels.

????

Something had happened today
The sky was clear and deeply blue
While the atmosphere tasted of sugar
And the wind, of mint
...cool

Even indoors, the sun was beaming shafts of warmth
Waking our two lovers, still in each other's arms
Their smiles echoed, affecting the outside world

As flowers glistened in full bloom
Trees reached up and painted the horizon
Birds harmonized, cars blended
And humanity drowned out

(except for our two lovers, still in each other's arms)

Day turned to night and with it came the moon
And oh, what a moon
Brighter than the sun, perfectly round
The expression on its face contradicting
Contradicting its full heart
And keeping our two lovers in each other's arms.

forevER

DOn't

                                                               saY

----------------------YOU

                                                                        LOVe

                                                                           me

_____<u>UnLeSS</u>

you mean it..please!!!!!!!

100

There once was a man
99 times he had tried
99 suicide attempts
only on the 100th did he get it right

he tried to drown
he slashed his wrists
overdosed on painkillers
but failed every time

number 50 involved food
number 28 required fire
66 summoned the devil
while 99 was just lazy

stranger they became
his desire to end his life
less people cared
"he'll never succeed" they said

then came the 100th
and the freedom he sought
and who would have thought that the 100th
was the simplest of them all

he just wished it.

Useful Quotes

If I am not noticed in life
how will I be missed in death?

All it would have took was for someone to listen

3 bottles of whiskey and a bag of ice
that's my shopping done for a week

Creativity has its price
that price is Absinthe

Fear your own mind

Why celebrate the day you were born into this world
that's just sick!

Should I kill myself now or later?

You only have 1 heart, so FUCK IT!!

Salvation is beyond saving

Don't judge my head before you have seen my heart

Don't embrace my heart until you have heard my head

There is no light at the end of the tunnel

Forgiveness is not possible

Revenge is the way

Suicide is the act of freedom

Suicide is my destiny

Fate dies.

GENeticcc

'"""""""""""""""""""""""""""""""ONee

                    suGGesTIon

is

                                    tHAT

                  depreSSion

                    is

                            GENetic
                            genETIC

        IN

                              ORigin"""""""""""""""""""""""""""

How Can Anyone Listen????

People
dislike
talking
about
DEATH
and
it
is
often
regarded
as
PSYCHOLOGICALLY
UNHEALTHY
to
want
to
do
so

"I DISAGREE"

Death and suicide or feelings of death and suicide are part of life and should be discussed and explored. If we don't talk about them, then how can anyone listen?!?!?!

DREAm

I had a dream that I died.
It was the best dream I have ever had.
It was also the worst.
Why?
Because I woke up and realised
it was just a dream.

StatistIC

Why do people
pretend to want me here?

Why do people
pretend to be my friends?

I am nothing.

I am no one.

I wouldn't want me
to be here.

I wouldn't want to
be my friend.

I am not even worthy
of being a memory.

I am not even worthy
of being a thought.

I am a statistic.

L
O
V
E

I
S

Love is the money you have worked for
Love is the plant you water
Love is the drink that gets you drunk
Love is the first note on your favourite album
Love is the itch that you scratch
Love is the lost child found
Love is the fly you free from the web
Love is the pillow and the duvet
Love is the up after the down
Love is that first phone call after that first date
Love is life after death
Love is the tack holding up the poster
Love is the unexpected twist in a film
Love is the spinning chair that makes you feel sick
Love is when a plan comes together
Love is the blank page filled
Love is a woman's belly button
Love is the satellite dish
Love is the trophy on the shelf
Love is the poem that writes itself

Love is the darkness
Love is the smell of a clean house
Love is the eagle on the par 4
Love is in the eyes
Love is in limbo
Love is having more time

L
O
V
E

I
S
?

Care For Me

The number of people who care for me is decreasing rapidly. Abrupt **stop**.

Fly With Them/////////////

What follows is what will end. Not in the form of poetry or short stories, but in the form of lyrics...an album. The Continuation Of Nothing.

1. Black
2. Dear Dad
3. PG
4. The Continuation Of Nothing
5. M(ultiple)umS(clerosis)
6. The Diner
7. A Verse From The Heart
8. Hurt
9. Once Upon A Time
10. A Dead Home
11. Point

Expression through words is as important as expression through music. These 11 songs are my gift to you, the reader, and the musician...fly with them.

Black

All the world has given up on me.
I make everyone go away in the end.
All the world has given up on me.
I make everyone go away in the end.
All the world has given up on me.
I make everyone go away in the end.
All the world has given up on me.
I make everyone go away in the end.
This world has failed me.
Everyone is gone.
Only one shade of black remains.

Dear Dad

The dripping alcoholic
The warm liar
The ageing sinner
The abusive man
The dead weight
The piercing fear
The blueprint
Like father, like son
Is this what I am to become?

The haunting
The shouting
The stealing
The anger
The pain
The smell
The blueprint
Like father, like son
Is this what I am to become?

Hate
Spit
Fight
Lost
Self
Destiny
The blueprint
Like father, like son
Is this what I am to become?

PG

Draw yourself a box and put yourself inside,
paint the walls black and fuck the entrance,
starve yourself of the love you deserve.
My pile is bigger than yours.

Suffocate the air and use it up,
become timeless cold to the touch,
crucify your values and bury their remains.
My pile is bigger than yours.

Deafen your conscience shut the fucker up,
final the resolutions that govern the norm,
soil the face reflected in the mirror.
My pile is bigger than yours.

Reveal the anger and pain that controls you,
scab wounds that lead to your salvation,
feed thoughts darkness captures with its fantasy.
My pile is bigger than yours.

Ink my blood
Lock away
Desire death
Loneliness
One.

The Continuation Of Nothing

Caged
Reduced to mindless
Restricted
Identities taken away
Become part of nothing
Shit on a stick
Paid with insult
Numb
Feel for hell
Time fucking vanishes
Lost
Time fucking merges
Unrecognisable
Same shit...different day
Isn't this madness?
Isn't this wrong?

Scraps
Looked down upon
Used
Life wasted away
The continuation of nothing
Fucking piss ants
Praise with lies
Cold

Feel for hell
Time fucking vanishes
Lost
Time fucking merges
Unrecognisable
Same shit...different day
Isn't this madness?
Isn't this wrong?

M(ultiple)umS(clerosis)

This chronic disease of the central nervous system can affect 1 person in 2000 in Britain. Multiple small scattered 'plaques'-areas of degeneration and loss of the insulating myelin sheath of nerve fibres-occur in a random manner anywhere in the brain or spinal cord. Where these plaques occur, the conduction of the nerve fibres is blocked and the function served by them is lost (FOREVER). As a result, those affected (MY MUM) develop a wide range of disabilities resulting from loss of nervous system function. This includes weakness, paralysis, loss of sensation, visual loss (IT STARTED IN HER EYES), severe lack of coordination and mental disturbances (SHE WASN'T CRAZY). The cause remains unknown and there is no effective treatment for MS (MUMS THE WORD).

The Diner

Shaking, nervous, slight
should I be alone?
left with my own mind
in a room of life
surrounded by black and white memories
conversations bouncing off the walls
bubbles rise
as fixed fans dream of escape
marble tables stain
and salt blinds my devil
or was it my angel?

The diner invites me
feeds off me, in me
holds me
the diner

50's music relaxes me
uncomplicated, fresh, dangerous
cocktails beckon my heart
beer soothes my belly
two lovers are lost
and I order dessert, banoffee sundae
sealed with a kiss
oh to be a stranger in love

The diner invites me
feeds off me, in me
holds me
the diner

The diner invites me
picks at me, through me
bleeds me
the diner
the diner.

A Verse From The heart

Tortured by the head
Beaten and raped
I scream for help
Beg for our soul
Cry...

I don't want to beat no more.

Hurt

And it's when I am totally alone
That I feel it the most

And it's when my own voice
Is all I can hear

I look around for something to do
I look around for any distraction

But it's too late

I become awash with pain
And covered in despair

My thoughts destroy me
My feelings darken
My strength fails
And...

Another piece of me is lost...
Forever.

Once Upon A Time

Hear the pin drop
Feel the blood fountain
Beautiful isn't it?
The smell of music
The taste of finality
The drum of suicide

Served on a bed of skin, locked in a cage of paint, surrounded by confessions of 'once upon a time'

Shine the light
Record the time
Sad isn't it?
The future lost
The ashes of dreams
The desire of suicide

Served on a bed of skin, locked in a cage of paint, surrounded by confessions of 'once upon a time'

Who was I? Good or bad?
I couldn't stand being reminded of what I didn't have
By those who had it.

No one has to ignore me any more
No one has to not care

Bury the coward
Curse the ignorance
Too late isn't it?
The tears of gutter
The guilt of betrayal
The 'once upon a time'

Served on a bed of skin, locked in a cage of paint, surrounded by confessions of 'once upon a time'.

A Dead Home

A lonely staircase full of faces
stained carpets tired and old
cracked ceilings frown
and floorboards complain
the wallpaper weeps dirty
as open doors now shut
a battered wardrobe
a tubeless TV.
A lifeless house...a dead home.

The coat hanger in the shower
rusted trophies fallen and disgraced
time devours proud brick
while wood replaces glass
it's heating heart now cold
it's bright head now dark
a legless table
a deaf icon.
A lifeless house...a dead home.

It listened.
It fed.
This was my pride, my life.
It screamed.
It drained.
This was my shelter, my kept.
It lived.
It died.
This was myself, my body.
A lifeless house...a dead home.

Point?

And oh, what a view.
An ideal spot...stained to be.

Everything done for the last time.
No more repetition.
No more boredom.
No more than a fading shadow.
A silent memory.
A single tear-drop.
Scripted to the last scene.
Destined to be.
There was never any escape.
There was never any point.

THE NOTE

THE END

Death is like an open book,
you just can't help but look,
for on it in big red letters it reads,
'The End'...after all, that's all it means.
?????

Thanks

First and foremost, the angel who saved me from the bottle and saves me from myself every day-Michelle McMahon.xxx

My sister, Joanne (wooood smooog) and her boyfriend Dave. The friends who have stuck with me through everything: Andrew Boyer (Moz), Chris Ratcliffe (Chrissy), Steven Gibson (Gibbo), Steven Wills (Wills), Derreck Nuttall (Metal God)...the greatest a man could ask for!

A special thank you to the entire Ainsworth family.

Other friends, family members and social networking fanatics.

Michelle's family: Jim, Caroline, Louise, Collette, Dixie, Fluffy.

To all I have worked with in Dean Wood Golf Club kitchens, Prepco Food Limited and Sanko Gosei.

To Grosvenor House Publishing Limited for being very patient and extremely helpful.

To the many writers, artists, musicians, directors and actors who have infuenced and inspired me throughout.

Finally, to my mum: you deserved better. To my dad: shame on you. And to my cat, Kitt: thank you.x

James S M Parker.

http://inbrokenthoughts.blogspot.co.uk

http://www.theeroticwoman.com/search/node/absintheangeldust

Tweet @absinthe666

Next – Life and Death

Remember – don't suffer in silence:

http://www.samaritans.org/

jo@samaritans.org

All profits made from this book will be donated to The Samaritans.

A final thank you to you, the reader – 09/06/12.

www.ingramcontent.com/pod-product-compliance
Lightning Source LLC
Chambersburg PA
CBHW032021040426
42448CB00006B/696